Limericks
of the
Lockdown

Limericks *of the* Lockdown

By

ROB WALKER

CONSCIOUS CARE PUBLISHING

Limericks of the Lockdown

First Published 2020 by: Conscious Care Publishing
PO Box 776, Rockingham, WA 6968, Australia
www.consciouscarepublishing.com

First Edition printed December 2020.

National Library of Australia Cataloguing-in-Publication entry:
Author: Walker, Rob
Limericks of the Lockdown / by Rob Walker
9780645089202 (Paperback)
9780645089219 (ebook)

Printed by Lightning Source
Typeset & cover design by Conscious Care Publishing

ISBN: 978-0-6450892-0-2

DEDICATION

For Carol

AUTHOR NOTES

Born a boomer in the suburbs in forty six
Walked barefoot to primary for an edufix.
High school was bland
Except for rock music land
Then to further studies for a Science mix.

Teaching was always my driven goal
So in Education I did enrol.
They filled this man
With a lifelong plan
And I embarked on a decades long role.

My family's story is written in this book
Open it up and just take a look.
It describes wife and flock
As domestic secrets unlock
I'm so content with the road that I took.

Rob

INTRODUCTION

We are experiencing a world pandemic. It is a very serious situation that has caused the loss of thousands of lives and is proving to be extremely difficult to control. Many elderly and front-line care givers are among those who have lost their lives. The infection has caused family and relationship strain and has undoubtedly placed people in mental states of anxiety, stress and depression. It is a truly awful virus that has changed the entire world.

I have chosen the Limerick form to convey my images because I can't write a novel and a limerick is only five lines long. That is about the limit of my concentration. At this point I would like to apologise to all Irish folk, past, present and future for taking their rhyme form to unforeseen places and for the use, and some would say, the abuse of the limerick form of expression.

My first limerick must give credit to the wonderful health workers around the globe who work endlessly and with great professional passion to address the needs and health requirements of those afflicted.

Health Angels

In the community they are pure gold,
Selflessly working at tending the fold.
With patience and calm
Neglecting self-harm,
Our health workers are out of God's mould.

With a lot of time on my hands, I have taken this diabolical situation, interpreted some of my activities and in the true Aussie spirit, added a small dash of humour. This has always been a way for Australians to cope with disaster and adversity. Paul Hogan's screen characters are the epitome of this situation. It may well be a coping mechanism that adjusts the mental state to a level where we can deal with great adversity.

High level lockdown of cities such as Christchurch and Melbourne were very serious levels of control. Together with isolation of the infected are the very strong measures needed to stop and reduce the increase of infections.

My slant on this-

Lockdown
If you are in lockdown LOCKDOWN.
That's 14 days and don't be a clown.
Stay 14 indoors,
Or 14 between floors
And you can still wear your hoodie dressing gown.

I would blame my diversions on Frost's "A Road Less Travelled" and hope we can achieve a truce via his work "Mending Wall." I do realise this is an Australian born "of Scottish heritage" using an American to explain deviances to the Irish nation!

Before starting my meagre collection of epics poetic can I finally confess that I believe the utterances of some international politicians have been truly diabolical. I believe most Australian politicians and their medical advisers have been excellent Some international political aspirants, I feel, are well summed up by the images presented by PB Shelley in Ozymandias. These I've called Polimandias.

I'm often asked "why the limerick form" and my answer –

Iambic pentameter doesn't get to me,
A sonnet's 14 lines just makes me flee.
Nothing's so neat
As 5 lines complete,
So I'll stick with the limerickology.

I hope you find some enjoyment in reading about my journey through the early days of the pandemic, that is Covid-19.

Jump in.

CONTENTS

Chapter 1

BEGINNING

The one that started it all. A few events into the lockdown I was feeling the angst. Forced to stay at home and not able to go out. I never used to go out a lot just at the supermarket and get fuel on cheap fuel Monday's. Now I here I was "forced" to stay in although the forcing was my own doing. I had slung a couple of limericks at a mate. He only returned with one and then out of the blue I constructed the "Marathon" and sent it. I continued with the limerick battle.

1. Marathon

Sex seventeen times again today,
I'm exhausted since the virus came to stay.
My back is so crook,
I need a good book
Or I'll leave this house horizontal on a tray.

I just pushed on with more limerick fun. I wasn't worried my work wasn't answered. I wasn't overly concerned about the quality and quantity of my work. I just had to write.

2. Limerick Battle

The limerick battle has just begun
What a hoot it's a barrel of fun.
This silly old fart
Has just made a start
The pearls of wisdom will now start to run.

The juices were flowing the words kept emerging – so many words – so many rhymes. A small word of warning about unsafe behaviour and keeping a safe distance and no cuddles.

3. Limerick Battle II

Limericks are much like a virus,
Unlimited words that'll not stifle us.
Stay away from each other,
No cuddle from mother
Just play the game with us and no fuss.

There was no battle. Only me driven to write by my perceived success. I checked my supply of writing material. My typing technique and speed would limit my frenetic output considerably – so longhand writing is the go. I do have a history of cursory writing. I was the ink monitor in Primary School, grade VI. Made the ink from powder and water, this to be used by a pen with nib. I'm now high tech so the ball point pen is the weapon of choice. On my first dash to the supermarket, I grabbed two packets of Kilometric Paper Mates. Sketches made with the old chewed HB pencil.

4. Writing Verse

Lying low in the house 'cos of virus,
Out of paper to write on so it's papyrus.
Pen and ink's running low,
So a lead pencil's the go
I hope the bug doesn't take out all of us.

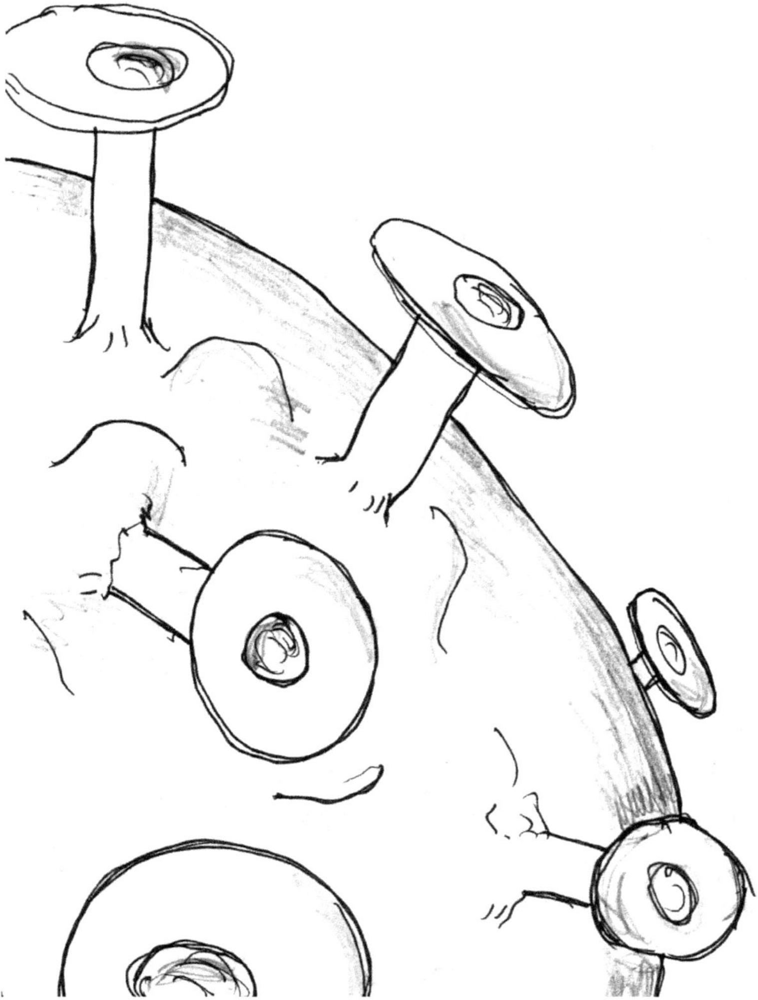

Chapter 2

THE LIMERICK

I am caught by the limerick bug but they're not all perfect. Some-times they have rhythm and some rhyme in time. Some rhyme tight and others give fright. Some are trite and some have insight. I write watching TV. I wake at night to write. I write like I'm possessed.

5. Limerick

A Limerick is my vehicle of choice
To raise issues that need a loud voice.
Shout it out now,
Stuff the sacred cow
And we can all stand up and rejoice.

I'm in the zone with the limerick. It's short, informative and melodic. There's a lot that can be said in five lines and few words together with creative images. Perfect for my short attention span.

Read – Think – Savour – Enjoy!

6. Limerick Rhyme

This is not all rhyming rubbish,
It's written with a great deal of flourish.
It takes a little time,
To find words that rhyme
And link them together and be bullish.

Its time to acknowledge the origins of the Covid-19 predicament. There is no doubt there's an association with the Wuhan Province in China but its exact beginnings may never be known.

7. Oriental Express

The virus from the East comes out real fast,
The reaction is not started at first cast.
Infection moves quick,
Doesn't miss a trick
And we need a solution that will last.

Covid-19 virus origins are similar to the SARS epidemic of 2002. The Severe Acute Respiratory Syndrome had no known transmission after 2004.

8. Virus Fight

The East may have virused us again,
First SARS now Corona causing pain.
Just mask up and gown
It will die down,
But the fight will now drive you insane.

Chapter 3

ALIENS

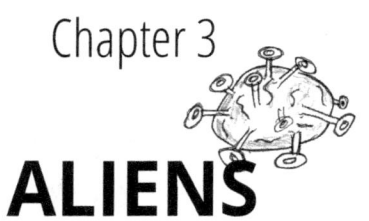

I always thought the one thing that would unite the whole world would be an alien invasion from an extra-terrestrial life form. All out wars and border problems and petty international bickering would totally cease as we addressed the common invader.

My introduction to aliens is a rather flippant one. It hints at more serious aliens to come.

9. Alien

Aliens come in pink, green and blue.
They might even land on me and you.
Clever little things,
No barbs or stings
Just don't get one stuck on your shoe.

There was a recognition that the alien had "landed" and was a serious adversary with deadly intent. There is a glimmer of hope offered that a vaccine may be possible. I have great faith in human ingenuity. There is massive development of possible vaccines with governments already negotiating possible supply lines and investigating dissemination routes. The human spirit will prevail.

10. Aliens

An alien came into my world today,
Surely hope it doesn't want to stay.
It'll rip you apart
From a stand-up start,
So we'll just have to vaccine it away.

The virus is now seen as a truly international spread. It moves through some nations more rapidly than others. Ships, planes and automobiles move people great distances and at high speed – how our alien spreads. There is no vaccination available a degree of isolation is required as a first basic step to slow the spread.

11. Alien Solution

The closest thing to an alien invasion,
Is a virus that influences every station.
Surging through a nation,
A vaccine needs creation
Then ultimately all of us are out of isolation.

Chapter 4

LOCKDOWN

It is now clear that certain groups of people are more susceptible to the virus than others. The elderly and those with compromised immune system are advised to take stringent methods of social isolation. Young people and kids appear to be less threatened. “Drawing the dark curtain” may be a grim thought but it is the feeling of the time. Unless aged care facilities are quickly developed into fully functioning ER centres there will be a potential for large numbers of casualties. This can’t happen so we have to do the best with what we have.

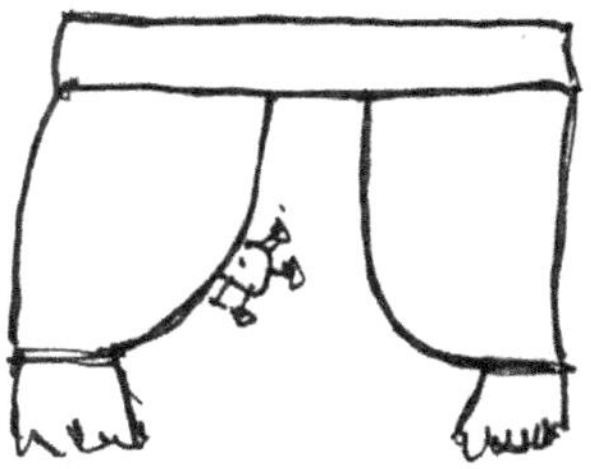

12. Start to Lockdown

Mums, kids and dogs are all roving outside,
But as an old person I'm required to hide.
Draw the dark curtain
Because nothing is certain,
And I think I'm in for a dizzying ride.

A mental aberration. I am fortunate that I have a small lawn and garden. Some people must spend a great deal of time in units and apartments, who have no external recreational area. There must be many who also have limited views from their home. I really have little to complain about compared to many others.

13. Lockdown

I only play in my backyard, I do.
I mow the lawn and tidy the edges too.
All the flowers I preen,
Though they're largely unseen
And I'd not be more-crazy locked in the loo.

Then there was lockdown of the more formal nature. Hotel rooms – some with opening windows and some without. Security and defence force personnel, and in some instances, police were employed to ensure compliance with the lockdown order. In Western Australia some retuning overseas tourists had to endure two weeks stay on WA's premier holiday island – Rottnest. This is home of the famous photogenic Quokka. All visiting celebs and sporting greats have the mandatory selfie with this cheeky looking marsupial. This is surely lockdown paradise.

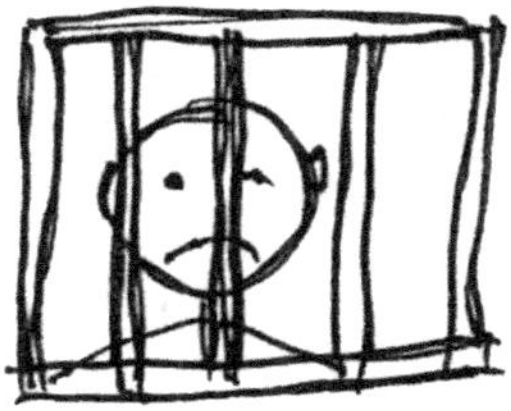

14. State Lockup

Lockdown is better called lockup,
One-way solitude and no backup.
Meals bore in,
Variety a sin
And I can't find an audience to speak up.

Lockdown for a single person has to be the hardest to endure. TV you learn to hate. Clocks are the enemy. A newspaper may be your new distraction for a while- you always wanted to master the cryptic crossword. It's not long before the TV is turned off, the clock gets covered and the only to solve craptic clues is to go to the paper to find answers to the previous day's questions.

15. Four Walls

Corona lockdown is my loneliest fate,
Eat, sleep and live without a mate.
Time goes slow
Many days to go,
The four walls enclosing me I hate.

Lockdown in your own home offers far more options for sane living. You have things and games and activities you have been putting off for years. Dig out those old jig-saw puzzles. Find out how to play Chess or Bridge or Mahjong or Poker. The internet is a great source of information. If you are bored then you are the solution. From Mind Numbing Entombment the only way is up. Get creative. Paint, sketch or write to or play remote Chess with a friend.

16. Mind Numbing Entombment

Lockdown under the military and police,
For a fortnight without early release.
Boring as drying paint,
Need patience of a saint.
Can't wait for entombment to cease.

Some people absconded from the lockdown regime. Top sportsmen and their coaches ventured away from lock-down. One inventive escapee used a supplied ladder to visit a partner for a nocturnal liaison. A lot of football players were caught going AWOL resulting heavy personal fines as well as massive fines for their respective clubs. Football has been different especially the AFL where there were very few spectators and the spectacle for those in lockdown was a "synthetic" crowd.

17. Silent Footy

AFL footy's all silent no crowd,
Recorded noise is played real loud.
Dial boos or cheers,
A sound engineer steers
And It's all pretend footy under a cloud.

The Covid-19 virus description and effects from a bug to a thug, and then compared to humanities greatest afflictions – drugs.

18. Virus

Covid-19 virus among us is a bug
It behaves throughout us as a thug.
We'll all fall down,
If we can't stop this clown
Its destruction is worse than a drug.

The virus growth is exponential. It accelerates increasingly. After a while it was more meaningful to show a graph of the data was on a logarithmic (log) scale on the Y axis (sorry for the maths lesson). If this scale wasn't used you would need a large piece of paper to represent some places, such as New York State, when it had hundreds of deaths a day.

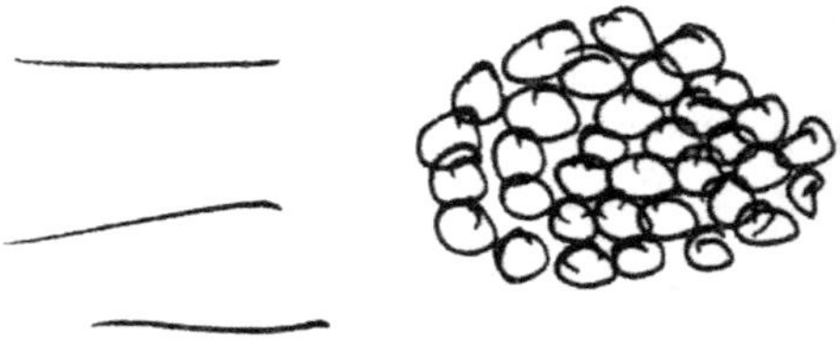

19. Virus Growth

The virus has sneaky multiplying tricks,
One contact then two and then six.
Exponential the growth,
No denial under oath
More crosses than a man's house has bricks.

There were some weird and wonderful treatments for corona. Some wacky and some down-right dangerous. I would like to propose an action that will maintain social distancing and is quite safe.

20. Better than bleach

A virus is a chemical and not a living thing.
We're safer if we separate and not closely cling.
Let's keep apart,
Launch a pretend fart
And people will not group together and sing.

Chapter 5

MASKS

Some people started wearing masks. They were in short-supply so large orders were made with overseas companies. The irony was not lost on me when huge orders for masks were made with Chinese suppliers.

I contemplated my own supplier. I have used their product before on home projects. They are cheap and durable. They have a metal strip to tighten on to the nose bridge and come the stark medical grade colour of white.

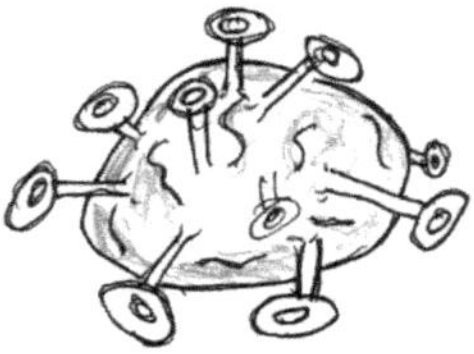

*Masks represented are not real and could cause harm. Use only Medical grade masks.

21. Mask

I just need to find a new facemask.
Can't locate one no matter who I ask.
Hardware ones are no good
They just filter wood.
I'll hold my breath, sit in the sun and just bask.

There were some weird solutions around for masks. Some people were sewing up masks from woven material. I saw some wearers where I made my very rare visits to the supermarket. Some had the full kit – mask, gloves and a packet of wipes in hand! The best effort for a mask was on YouTube. A woman was demonstrating how position a thong (undergarment) over her head and face! Not a good look. My offering is tongue in cheek – well not literally.

22. Mask Solution

I need to find a new facemask real quick,
They're too thin, just right or too thick.
Cut up pantyhose,
Shove tight up your nose
It keeps the virus out that's the trick.

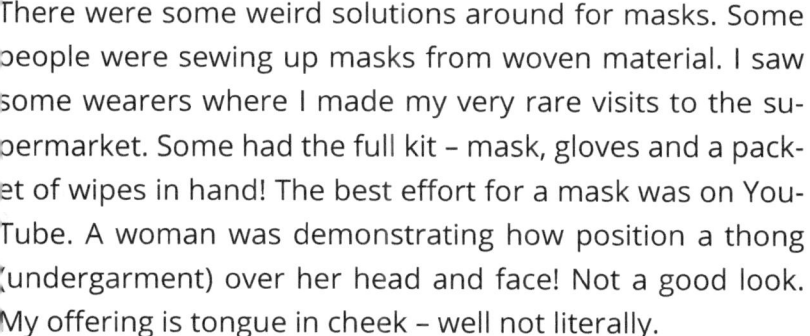

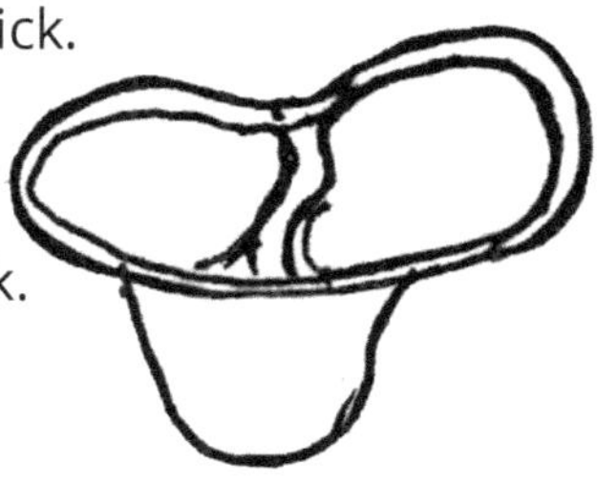

Masks are pretty standard devices. A rectangle of appropriate material with two loops of elastic to loop over your ears. Noses, mouths and chins are fairly standard issue. What have noticed is that there is a great variation, not only in the shape and size of ears, but in the many tasks we now have our "head handles" do for us. We hang all manner of ornaments on them. We pierce then. We stretch the lobes. We hang buds in them to allow us to hear our music and we crush them many times a day with a mobile phone. We are now required to hang a mask on them.

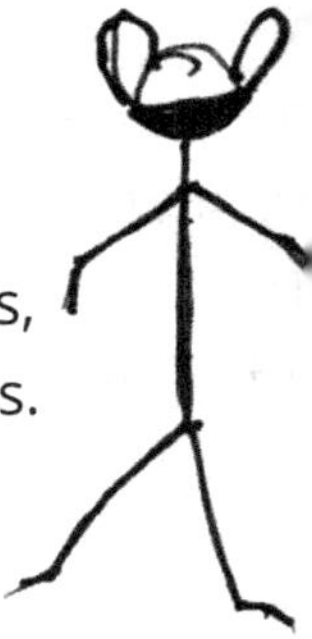

23. Ears

Some people's ears are just better for masks,
Pixies, dumbos and some like bungs in casks.
Hang it on tight,
Give the virus a fright
Didn't know your ears had other major tasks.

There are other sources of materials from which to make your mask. Be inventive. Search around and use your imagination. One unexplored source is again an item of clothing that can be adapted for our cause and to make the 'Home-made Mask"

24. Homemade Mask

Use a bra to fashion your masks,
It should be shared with anyone who asks.
A double D will do
One bra will make two
And you'll have a great mask for all tasks.

Down the hardware store again for some more items to construct our next Budget mask. Some of these items come in a variety of colours so they will be in demand as a fashion accessory.

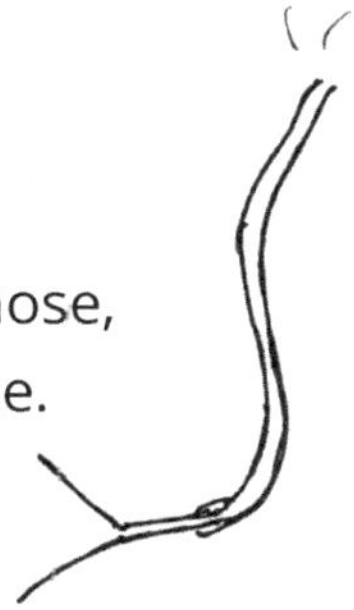

25. The Funnel Mask

A plastic funnel will cover mouth and nose,
It's a snorkel with a short length of hose.
Up in clear air,
It's safer up there
Just breathe out slowly and the air flows.

Another fashion accessory that can be utilised as a functioning mask is the humble drinking straw. They come in a variety of colours and materials. There are paper ones for the environmentally conscious although these may become soggy with extended use and have to be discarded prematurely. Plastic ones come in a variety of colours and it's your choice as to whether you want to mix or match the colours to enhance your ensemble. There is, of course, the ever popular plain black straw. These are a huge hit with the cocktail set and complement well with the little black dress or a young man's after five wear.

26. Straw Mask

Drinking straws up nostrils look great,
With intra cotton wool the virus will abate.
Breathe in real slow,
The virus will go
And a great result will just be your fate.

Glass funnels are available. Science equipment suppliers and, perhaps, homewares shops may sell them. Several layers of material held over the end with an elastic band would be the filter and the whole filter device could be washed when required.

27. A Glass Funnel Mask

A small funnel can make an ideal mask,
Have a coffee using the end in a flask.
For smokers a godsend,
With the cigarette in end
And it's good for a Sherry from a cask.

And for the young entrepreneurs and go getters there is the large untouched world of advertising. Don't waste the space. You are out there in people's faces – so to speak. Your mask space has value and so does the thousands of other masks that that are being worn in the public domain. You can be the first to monopolise this new and unique advertising space.

28. Mask Ads

Adverts on masks is what shows.
Pay people to sign coffee that goes
"Eat Steak at Joe's",
"High Tea at Floe's"
A large sign will cover your mouth and nose.

Glass masks are 100% recyclable and can be washed and , indeed, polished to a high level of sheen. For the truly artistic there is also the Tiffany Lamp look when leadlight is incorporated into the design.

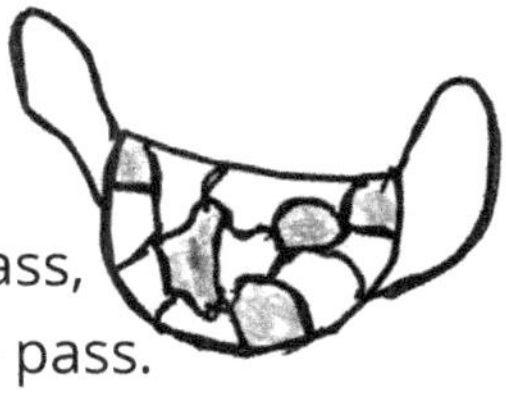

29. Glass Mask

A mask could be made out of hard glass,
Wash off phlegm, gooz, spit and nose pass.
It's clear as day
To see through OK.
And lead light would make it real class.

Chapter 6

THE IMPOSTER

Its presence keeps affecting me. It's here, it's worldwide and all of humanity is involved. International cooperation and communication are required. Is finding blame helpful? There has been strong condemnation of China by President Trump and to a lesser degree by our own Prime Minister. Trade relations are suffering as a result of this international disharmony. The fractured international relations appear now to be some distance from the original misunderstandings.

30. Imposter

A great imposter this Corona Virus.
Its impact has affected near all of us.
Seen in Wuhan,
Affecting all of man
We have to get rid of it without a real fuss.

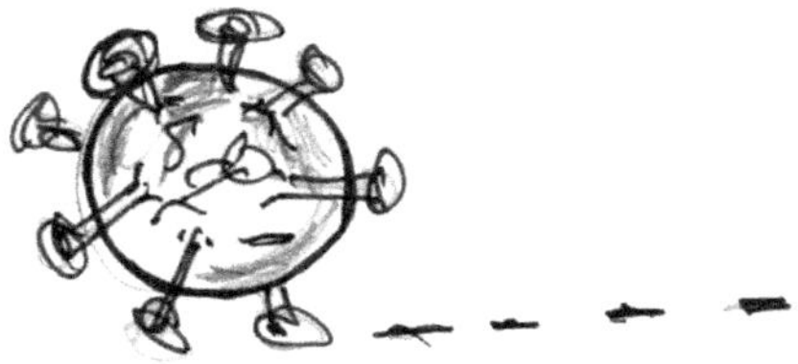

We all have constant reminders how to correctly wash hands, keep a social distance and greet people with safe gestures. There are constant reminders in supermarket aisles and on shop floors with messages about social distancing and even indicating a preferred direction of travel within the shop.

Greeting no longer involve handshakes and hugs. I find foot to foot and elbow to elbow greetings are great icebreakers and lead straight into wonderful communications. The "body language" of power handshakes will now need a whole new investigation. A stationary or moving elbow, or one moving forward, may indicate a degree of dominance compared to a drooping elbow. A great research area for someone in lockdown.

31. Its Name

It is Corona, Covid-19 or just a plain bug,
If you catch it you will be in a fug.
It can land in you space,
Attach to hands, arms or face
Keep clean and distant and don't be a mug.

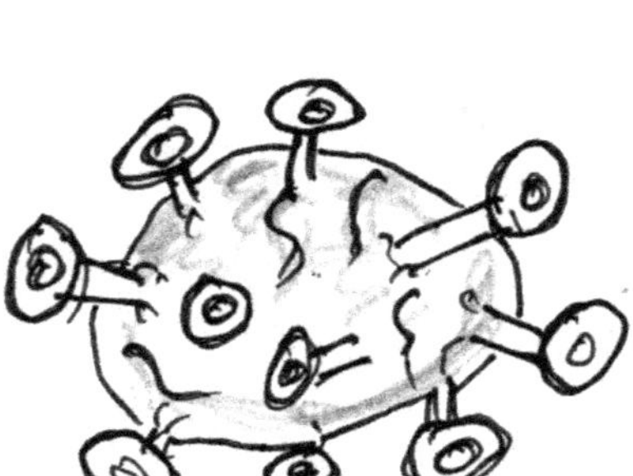

Chapter 7

ALONE TOGETHER

There is a degree of aloneness with the Covid-19 pandemic. In a sense we are all playing a singles game in the world arena that's conducting the game. Each of us must take responsibility for our actions. We are each responsible for every other person with whom we come in contact. This is a team game. We are all on the same team and we must all play by the same rules. I have developed this overwhelming feeling of connectedness with everyone. Community spirit is definitely alive (except toilet roll buyers!).

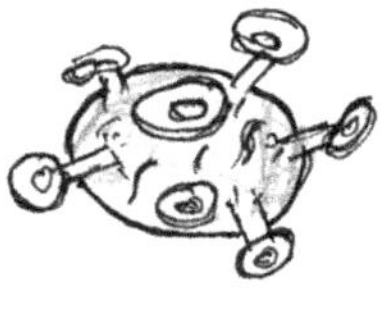

32. Alone

You are not alone in this virus mess
Though we see each other less and less.
You're always in mind
And a solution they'll find
There will be a release from this Corona stress.

And in the same vein as Alone, I was in lockdown in Autumn and that proved to have had a great calming influence. Spring and summer may have been harder in lockdown – half the world didn't have a choice. Autumn is a gentle time. We are slowly easing out of the intense heat and bushfire season to a more relaxed weather period. "Keep Calm and Carry On"

33. Autumn

Autumn is a season of great calm,
Safe at home without fear of harm.
Keep environments sterile,
Counteract the viral
We have to battle the threat without alarm.

We were all encouraged to download a smart phone app that would enable "authorities" to track and identify people who were close enough, and for long enough, to possibly be infected. I believe virtually all discovery of newly infected people is being done by a massive testing program. Am I wrong?

34. Covid App

Just downloaded the Covid-19 App,
Been encouraged to get this Covid trap.
Keep the phone on
Virus is not gone
And nobody is telling me if it's truth or just pap.

Just something to think about on a quiet Autumn eve.

Chapter 8

SHOPPING

There was a great deal of panic buying in the initial stages of the pandemic (panicdemic?). Stores were raided for toilet paper, bags of rice and pasta of all shapes and sizes. There was a run on cans of easy meal material such as soups and stews. Hand sanitizer was particularly hard to find. There was news footage of mature women fighting over the possession of large packs of toilet paper. Crap behaviour!

35. Shop Fight

Down at Woollies and hoping to score
Hand gel, loo paper and then out the door.
Gentle matrons are worse,
They hit with the purse
And you're lucky you're not trodden to the floor.

Sometimes I just want to annoy the person with the four giant packs of toilet paper in their trolley. I don't want to get physical or enter a verbal altercation so maybe a little play-acting is the way. (only kidding)

36. Easy Shopping

Gloved and masked wipe all the fruit down,
Sniffle, cough and sneeze make them all frown.
Stand near their cart
They'll soon depart,
This germ-free Woollies shopper is no clown.

There's a way to avoid all the shopping hassles. A phone, a credit card and patience. Shopping is so much more than just acquiring foodstuffs and material things. Shopping is tactile. Shopping is social. Shopping is filled with sights sounds and aromas. You can greet people, meet friends and maybe have a coffee and cake. I hope these days return soon.

37. Online Buying

I'm avoiding all shops at this time,
All my purchases are now being made online.
Key in your needs
Sew the monetary seeds,
You'll just grow all your debt just real fine.

The government announced that alcohol supplies were to be limited. A few day's notice was given which caused a mini run by the public to build their grog supplies. When the sanctions started, the queues were long yet spaced. Determined buyers could return for another purchase or even travel to another outlet. The amount available for purchase was over generous. Sales figures for liquor outlets must have been very good in the limited time the restrictions were in force.

38. No Booze

I'm battling the queue at the grog shop.
They come in racing and running non-stop.
Only want a little wine
To help pass the time,
But the only thing left is Alcopop.

The alcohol limit of purchase only lasted a short while and then normal buying habits returned. Trolley loads evenly spaced as they rolled out the door.

39. Dinner

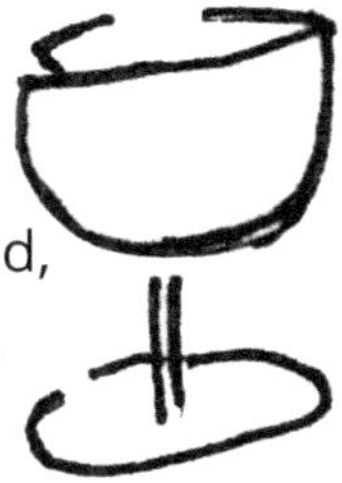

The pandemic's alcohol limit has just shifted,
My lifestyle standards are now again lifted.
I fancy a small wine
But only when I dine,
So to much earlier dining times I've just drifted.

Chapter 9 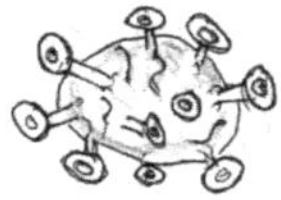

MUSICAL NOTES

Enjoying music is a great way to go in a pandemic. Soothing relaxing and provokes great memories. Depending on your age and whether you updated your gear or just threw it out, you could-Vinyl it, C.D. it, Cassette it, radio it, playlist it, or, stream it. It's all available and easy to get. In lockdown it's a bonus.

40. Best Music

Cancelled background noise with headphones today,
All my good music I managed to play.
None of your crap
Certainly no rap
'Cos great sixties music is just here to stay.

What more do I have to say. Like most people, strong music tastes are developed in your young years. This was time when you learned to memorised and appreciated the style and lyrics of the day. You wouldn't be able to afford the C.D. or L.P until much later. The Beatles arrived when I was in high school. With my music, I can get back to that anytime at all.

41. My Music

I spent years listening to songs with clear lyrics,
Not like today's songs from those oddball mystics.
Old rhymings are crisp
Sung without a lisp,
Sixties music is where I still get my kicks.

Play your music and challenge yourself with Shazam. Select a radio station or streaming service and work-out the artist, the name of the song, the year it was a hit and even the artist's age. (Maybe if they are still alive!) Am I starting to enjoy

lockdown?
Here I am
-Gardening
-Limericking
-Musicing
-Making up words
What's the opposite of cabin fever?

42. Shazam

How great is it life's just like Shazam,
Collecting song words from every woman and man.
Rock, blues and pop,
It will never stop
It's great music for this old rock fan.

Helpless? No I've regressed. Unable to visit or be visited so I tried to sit down and write a little verse. Keeping it together in lockdown can, at times, be quite fragile.

I am not depressed
I am not depressed
I am not
I am...

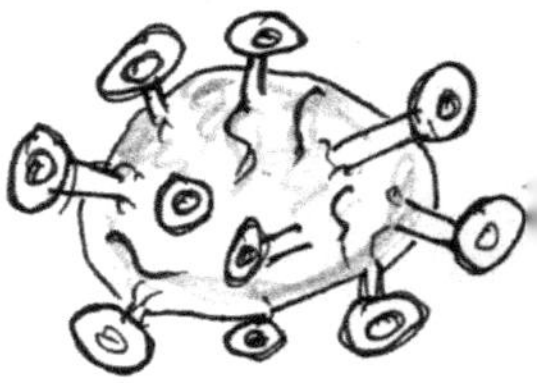

43. Helpless

Written in the evening when the wine does flow,
I believe like Scomo, have a go get a go.
I have nought
To give the virus a clout,
I'll just sip here and stare at my big toe.

Blues is better than booze. Music is great for the soul and great for the sole soul. Rekindle your true music loves. I have to fight the gloom and gladden up the room. Music. Some local libraries have a great collection of donated CD's. I have used this source on occasions and it's a cheap way to sample artists unknown to you. Give it a try when libraries open again.

44. See The light

Ailing sadness hardship and bad news,
Collect feelings from the greats of the blues.
BB and Hooker can lead,
To satisfy my need
And gospel Elvis will have us all sitting in pews.

I love the idea that a gold C.D. recording of "Johnny B Goode" was sent out on the voyager program. At present, it's about

19 billion kilometres out and still going. If an alien lifeform discovers our sent information, they'll hear some great rock music. Go Johnny go!

45. Limerickology

Limerickology is a term I love to use,
Thanks Chuck for the new words I give yuse.
The rhymes are all tight
From dark into light,
Damn the fooderator has just blown a fuse.

Chapter 10

EASTER

Easter in lockdown had me wondering if Covid-19 would cross species and into another mammal-the rabbit. I'm sure he(or she) is perfectly safe from that particular virus, but there are other hurdles for our furry friend.

46. Easter Bunny

It's Easter again and we welcome the bunny.
It finding us in lockdown is quite funny.
Eggs at the gate?
Delivery never late,
But a Calici hit would make life less sunny.

I've worked out why I didn't get Easter eggs this year. This is the time of the Virus. Mammals beware.

47. Poor Bunny

The Easter Bunny didn't make it this year,
To find out his fate lend an ear.
Nearly eaten by a cat,
Then Calici laid it flat
No eggs this year so I'll have a beer.

I try to stitch together a range of ideas that encompass interesting and entertaining situations. Then came along – the limerick lament.

Have a go and help me with the last line. End it with tap, lap, pap, yap or whatever. I've already used the word crap so find another one.

48. The Limerick Lament

Some limericks are good some are crap,
I try to rhyme stuff that's not pap.
Some words do rhyme
Each and every time

Chapter 11

MEDICO

Some things just have to be done in lockdown. There was an easing of lockdown restrictions and my dentist opened for appointments. I made a "worse case" prediction for my situation but all that was required was a scale and clean.

49. Dentist

Went down for my biannual teeth check,
Cleaned all the teeth that are gummed up to heck.
Ready for the drilling
And inevitable filling,
Cost a fortune this time 'cos they are a wreck.

Medical consultations are being undertaken via an online connection. Phone the doctor book a time so they have your records when you are communicating. The system is pretty good for most ailments except temperature, blood pressure and broken bones. Very confidential conversations may be a little difficult. Do you really trust the on-line experience?

50. Doctor Who?

I phone consulted with my doctor just fine,
They can't squeeze and prod things when online.
I do the tests,
With results he just jests
Did nothing for me and my bent spine.

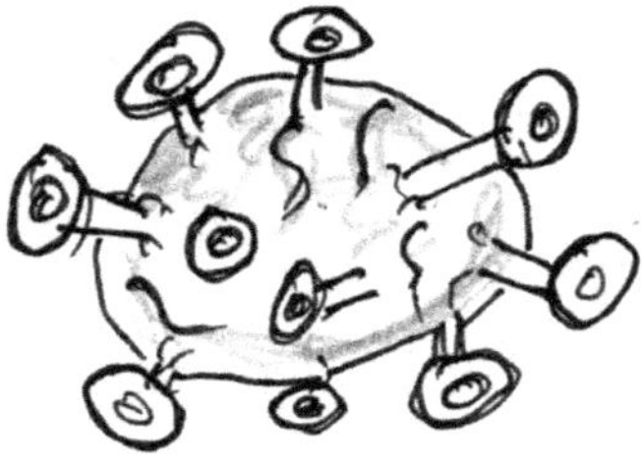

Chapter 12

FAMILY

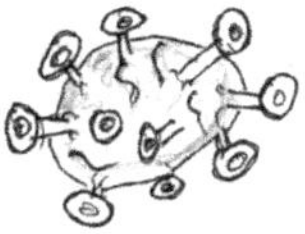

Just found a moment to count my blessings. Time is something you find you have in lockdown.

51. Family

Found a good woman and married...then,
Settled down and had three girls ...when,
They grew up strong,
Then came along
A bunch of grandkids numbering ten.

There are a lot of things you miss when social restrictions are in force. The family gatherings, Bar-B-Qs and picnics. You don't realise how social we are until restrictions are imposed.

52. Kids Help

The Bar-B-Q is the place to be,
Grandkids watching at your knee.
They can turn snags
Without being dags
How good they'll all turn out we'll just see.

Separated meetings are only marginally better than Facetime or Zoom. Talking through the door or waving through the window have become usual practice. Leaving gifts at the gate is another non-contact meeting. Grandkids birthdays are the worst. The promises of a later celebration doesn't seem to cut it. The separation situation for some people is diabolical.

53. Separation

Visited the grandkids today at their home,
Gifts exchange but felt all alone.
Waved from afar
As we left in the car
Virus clouded meetings are all cold as stone.

Little ones wearing floatation jackets doing "cannon balls" into the pool. The bigger ones doing bombies trying to empty it. All not happening. There is nothing more exciting than seeing a pool being used for maximum enjoyment. Young kids and water just go together and I am so thankful that mine is not..

54. Missing Them

Just been outback to clean the pool,
Sucked, brushed and scraped with a special tool.
The chlorines all set,
Acids a sure bet
Sad grandkids aren't around to act the fool.

My wife is wonderful putting up with me, especially with all the confines of lockdown. She's a retired health professional so safe anti-virus behaviours are all the go. I'm a very fortunate patient.

55. Home Care

I'm living at home in a one bed ward,
The matron's a good sort and I'm never bored.
The bed pan is warm,
Late rise from the dorm
Can't believe in lockdown how well I have scored.

Chapter 13

FOOTBALL

Live football ceased. At time of writing there was no live football games played in Australia. Television channels broadcast past recorded matches. In a lot of cases the matches chosen were the past glories of local teams. These were games where the result was in doubt up to the last minutes of the match. It was better than nothing and you may have even forgotten the past match and its result. (possible at my age).

56. No Footy

Footy's all stopped now we are all glum,
We're all tears including your mum.
Replays are it
They're still full of grit,
We watch it 'til the live stuff does come.

The commercial television stations don't miss a trick. There was a whole new range of advertising in and around the football broadcasts. Even the game breaks had their fair share of adverts. At whatever level of lock-down you are in the broadcasts still provide a diversion.

57. Footy Still

Footy re-runs are on the TV again,
Watch them and try to keep sane.
My team has a win,
Designed to keep me in
It's TV to mortify the brain.

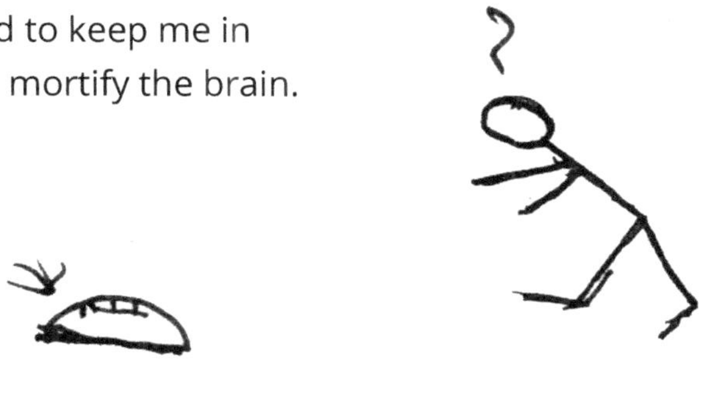

Chapter 14

PLANNING & PAINTING

And now for a quiet moment. This could be my RUOK self-assessment time. There is a serious side to lockdown apart from the very real behaviours needed to control the spread of a deadly disease. Quiet reflection can put some thoughts in order. Electronic communication with family and friends might prove very rewarding. Sometimes...peace.

My private moment will include something I never do. I'll have a footbath. Glorious.

58. Feet

I never use my old i-phone to tweet,
My private life is quiet and discrete.
I'm sitting here at home,
Composing a new tome
While relaxing here and soaking my feet.

The plan is to have a plan. There is always a list of things to do, things to mend and things to make. I make a long list of things that need my attention. Every conceivable thing I need to do around the home, new tools I need to buy and even minor and major maintenance that's required all go on the list. As each job is completed it is crosses off the list. Any new items that occur are added. Love it or hate it the list is always there.

59. The Plan

I've turned into the maintenance man,
Turning my hand to whatever I can.
I am no fool
Can use many a tool,
As long as I'm following my wife's plan.

I hate painting. I hate the preparation. Clear the room and move the furniture out. Hangings off walls. Cover the floor. Remove handles and locks from doors. And now the big

ones.
What type of paint? flat, matt, low sheen, semi- gloss, gloss
Is it water based or will I need turps?
Will I need a brush or a roller?
Have I patched all the cracks and holes?
How many coats are needed?
Do I need masking tape and what sort?
Calculate how much paint you need. Areas of walls minus doors and windows Add it all up.
Cost??? Have you checked the price of paint lately?

60. Painting Blues

Grandad is again on the paint brush,
House painting turns your brain to mush.
Roll it on thick,
Make the new coat stick.
No loud noises 'cos I need the hush.

I find that you never get away with only one coat. No matter what the colour its two coats. Cut in all the corners and edges. Do you use a ladder and move it along every metre? The ceiling is special. Rest your head back on your spine and paint the ceiling with a roller on a stick. Fight your unnatural muscle motions and gravity at the same time. I hate painting ceilings.

61. Painting

I'm bored stuck home here with the wife,
It's calm and I keep out of strife.
I don't have a vice,
Just paint things thrice
So it's no Bunnings while the virus is rife.

How many edges to paint in a room? Solution: walls, ceilings, doors - everything one colour. Now there's cleaning up. How much water to clean a paint roller? Thank goodness for disposable ones.

In lockdown I painted three bedrooms, a laundry, a bathroom, a toilet and a walk-in cupboard. That's empty the room, prepare all the surfaces, mask stuff, lay drop sheets and then paint. Now all the furniture goes back in.

62. Paint

Sitting alone in lockdown is a pain,
Made a "to do" list 'til I'm up and free again.
Jobs are getting done
Bunnings lines are gruesome,
Guess I'll paint my rooms again, again and again.

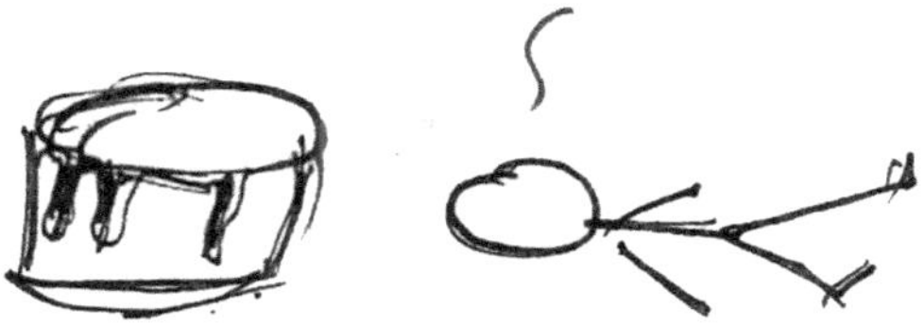

Chapter 15

TELEVISION

TV is available in lockdown. For a small outlay the choices are endless. There are a huge supply of movies from which to choose. In fact you can get very picky and make a decision very quickly as to whether the movie meets your standards. Flick it off. Try another. Oh a small red line shows I've rejected this previously. You find quite a number have been rejected very early. Picky in lockdown!

Then you discover programs with series. Three series-each with eight one hour episodes. The binge has arrived. Starts in 12 seconds...11...10...the countdown goes on. Will I go to bed?...9...8...7...I'll pick this up tomorrow...6...5...4...It has been good...3...2...1...It's started. OK one more episode.

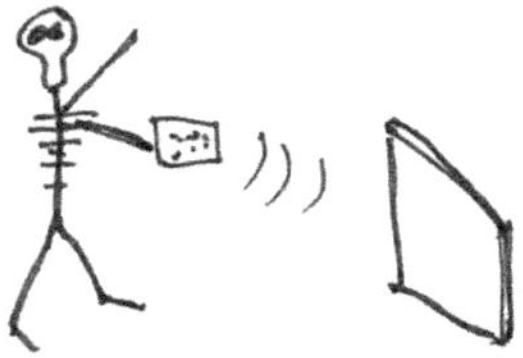

63. TV Blues

The viewing is again on the binge,
Murder, mayhem and zombie cringe.
For hours on end
I consume what they send,
Mish mash material that makes you unhinge.

Watch...eat...watch...drink...watch...doze...wake up...watch... rewind...watch the bit you missed. I'll watch just one more episode!

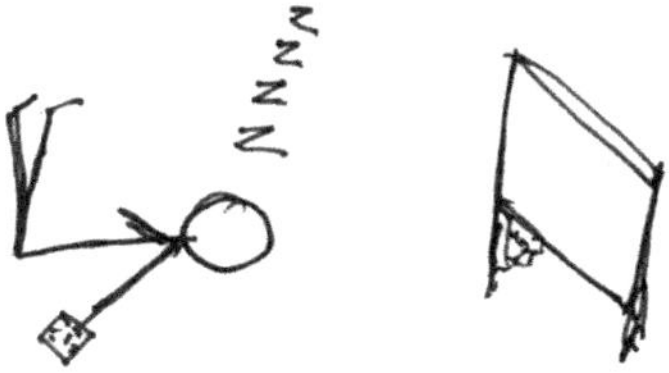

64. TV Binge

Growing fat watching TV on a binge,
Watching anything including the fringe.
No matter the show
I'll give it a go,
I'm not bored and I don't want to whinge.

Forget TV, Lego is the way to go. Lego is brilliant for some. You can make a composite vehicle from 200 small bits. As long as you build in sequence and don't miss any steps or drop any bits, a final product is yours.

I've seen the smallest kid follow non-verbal instructions and build the most complex structure. Adults engage in Lego builds and Ikea builds! We know how some of these turn out. Not me. I'll write instead.

65. Lego Anyone

I sit at my desk and write limericks,
Shuffling terms and finding new word tricks.
The pen does move fast
Making verse that will last,
Better than making Lego models from small bricks.

Chapter 16

LOCKDOWN DREAMS

In lockdown you can talk to plants-they understand-especially the flowers. Grass tends to ignore you as you just walk all over it. It's the wrong time to prune but you just do it anyway. It's easy to know when to stop – when you are down to sticks.

66. Lockdown

A garden needs pruning to grow,
Sharpen secateurs and give it a go.
Chop, cut and snip
Trim, edge and clip,
In a frenzy just go with the flow.

Looking out the back window there are three kookaburras on the back fence. Great look great sound. Takes me back to the Movietone News theme.

67. Kookaburras

Kookaburras are on the back fence again,
Their laughter's loud and drives you insane.
They dive in the pool
To be dustless and cool
I hope they stay much longer and drain.

Chapter 17

LOTTO

There was a marked increase in online gambling during lockdown. My only gambling vice is Lotto. The odds of winning are millions and millions to one. I buy, not invest, a minimum amount in some jackpotted games. This is sometimes only one game for a dollar or so. It's done online to save embarrassment at the local newsagent.

68. Lotto Dream

Lotto ap again says "Sorry, not a winner"
My hopes are dashed for being a grinner.
The tickets are bought
But all done for nought,
So its toast and jam for me again for dinner.

Never mind. Sitting at home in lockdown with a lot of money would be a pain. Buying all that stuff on-line and having it pile up at the front door.

69. Lotto Win

I think I've won Powerball today,
e-mail says there's 5 mill on the way.
I finally picked the balls
After so many falls,
S%#@ just woken up to a brand new day.

Chapter 18

KEEPING ACTIVE

Duck out and have a quick walk. Saunter round the neighbourhood, wave to people and shout greetings. Dodge anyone coming your way. Some coming toward me even cross the street. It's the virus it's the virus.

70. Exercise

For exercise I walk round the hood,
It's kilometres and it's all for the good.
Step up and down
Fit feet to crown,
It's great my shoes are not made of wood.

I'll get some exercise in the garden. It's the wrong time to plant stuff but I'll give it a go anyway. Recent panic buying did include seed packets. They must have bean planning for the long haul.

71. Crop

If the limericks do grind to a stop,
Means I've picked up the virus and do flop.
I'm stuck here at home
With only TV and phone,
Thinking of getting seeds and planting a crop.

I rode around Uluru a few years back on my electric bike. No. I pedalled all the way because it was flat. I treat it as a normal bike and always ride when I'm on level surfaces but there is no such thing as a hill. My wife and I fold the bikes up into the back of the ute and take them everywhere. (a little help at 74).

72. Electric Bike

I love my little electric bike,
I can wheel it and not have to hike.
It zooms all around
Covers lots of ground,
A full battery at the back is what I like.

The bike is the ultimate social distancer. Choose your route and choose your time. I did have a regular bike once (bought at a Police auction). Because I live in a particularly hilly neighbourhood, I would avoid taking it out. It went on the verge for someone else.

73. Bike

I ride my bike around the town,
Push it up hill over and down.
It is a neat little unit,
Just jump on and ride it
Past all of the green fields and brown.

Dreaming of another way to avoid painting and gardening. Drive. Take the long way to the supermarket or go to a less busy smaller grocery outlet. Plan the journey to include a Pharmacy visit when appropriate.

74. Driving Me Crazy

I could drive around all day in my car,
I'd escape the virus and wouldn't drive far.
Don't meet other folk
No shove, push or poke,
'Cos I'm no virus fool now I'm a star.

I have a section in the garage the grandkids call the "fixing room". They can hammer nails into softwood, drill holes with electric and hand drills with help and glue scrap pieces together to make masterpieces to take home. They cut wire to make bangles and drill gumnuts to string together to make necklaces. There a few ancient concrete garden gnomes that are always in need of a spruce up with a lick of paint. Gluing things together is always a favourite. Recently Mini Mouse needed both her head and nose reattached. I'm in there now alone with the tools.

75. Idle

I have hours idle throughout the day,
To sit, walk and talk and to stay.
I know my room well
The toys familiar as hell,
And daily I put my playthings away.

Chapter 19

POLITICS

Covid-19 is a Pandemic. It's a worldwide phenomenon. Every country is potentially part of the pandemic. Leading politicians within those countries is now responsible for their country's actions in putting in place criteria to minimise the harm to their people. Some countries appear to be doing better than others.

76. Politics

The mistakes of Boris and Trump are rife,
They have botched things up and are in strife.
Wish washy stabs
For reporters' grabs,
Is a thick fog you can cut with a knife.

People started dying in large numbers. Refrigerated trucks and commandeered ice rinks were being used to store the deceased. When the deaths in New York reached enormous numbers a day the magnitude of the pandemic got to me. Here is the greatest city in the world, in arguably the most advanced country in the world, with death figures that are hard to believe. My solution is unreal. So is this mess. I offer an unbelievable solution.

77. Solution

If you pushed your earbuds up your nose,
The dangerous virus might not have arose.
New York is so sad,
The virus is bad it's bad.
We'll scare it away with saltwater and a hose.

People I know in the UK are not impressed with the management of the Pandemic. Forever rising numbers of infections and a large number of deaths.

78. UK Politics

Boris acts like a bumbling buffoon,
No direction from Lands-End to Dunoon.
Masks on or off?
Hats on or doff?
Infections are going up like a balloon.

Helping out, an Australian businessman, would donate millions of doses of hydroxychloroquine (an untried Corona medication) to Australia. Donald Trump mentioned disinfectant, light and possibly bleach as solutions to test against the Covid-19 virus.

79. Buddies

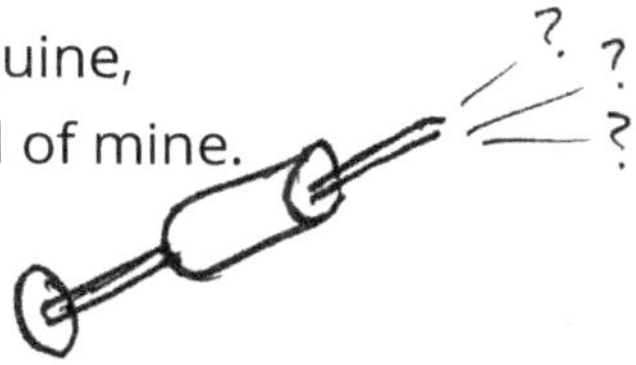

An old Aussie likes hydroxychloroquine,
World Leaders would say he's a pal of mine.
But disinfectants the way
Inject it or spray
Cocktail it with bleach and you'll be fine.

Some world leaders are getting aggressive towards the World Health Organisation. I don't believe that is very constructive. I did have to tone the language on this one.

80. WHO

"A leader" has taken on the WHO,
He wouldn't know what songs they do.
He acts like a fool,
"He's really not cool"
The bad, bad virus just shows him up woo, woo.

New York deaths due to Covid-19   25000 to date. One New York doctor called it "something out of a horror film" USA death toll to date 220 000. I change this figure every time I review this text.

81. A leader's Way

The leader stumbles and bumbles his way,
When New York has untold deaths in a day.
Logic down the drain
He's off base again.
Its not fake news when he has it his way.

Some leaders say the most bewildering things. They say and do things that are out of synch with their health advisors. This is improving.

82. Intelligence

Leader's intelligence appears to be only average,
From the way they speak on TV coverage.
The bad, bad press
Causes much duress,
In solving world events they're on the wrong page.

Donald Trump suggested that in America they test for Covid-19 far too much.

83. Virus Test

Trump tested positive in the most negative way,
His speech a roundabout twist to say.
Some things are very bad
True meanings are so sad
Because it's all Obama's fault anyway.

A great sorrow both times.

84. Great Sorrow

9/11 put three thousand souls down,
Now Covid-19 has come into town.
U.S.A. is a mess,
260 000* no less
As a total loss they hold the crown.

*At time of writing

And then there is sarcasm with advice coupled to help solve the situation.

85. Sarcasm

He's sarcastic with his tongue in his cheek,
True virus numbers he doesn't want to seek.
Don't do the test,
Our numbers will be best
And we'll show all deaths are of the weak.

Boris is a world leader and he's always in the news. He stumbles and bumbles around you'd think he'd know what to doos. Sorry. He's out meeting and greeting people, giving speeches and shaking hands. Oops. Boris becomes infected with Covid-19. This on top of just becoming a new dad.

Britain is not travelling well with increasing numbers of Covid infections and a return to more severe lockdown conditions.

86. Boris

Boris is a dad and we're so glad,
A new parent at 50 can't be that bad.
Nappies on the line,
New speeches taking time
Getting only half his sleep that is so sad.

Chapter 20

THE VIRUS CONTINUES

Despite the helpful and sometimes unhelpful advice from politicians, the infections continue and the numbers inevitably rise.

87. Silent Virus

No weeping sores or falling down in the street,
Covid-19 is quite silent and discrete.
Cross infection is fast
Symptoms now last
And passing infections to a population is now fleet.

Passing the virus through our breathing activity is how it is passed. Wearing a mask largely inhibits the flow of particles to or from our faces. Coughs and sneezes are largely impeded.

There is no immediate announcement of infection and it can take many days before symptoms become apparent.

88. Slow Attack

Covid-19 doesn't knock you down in the dust,
It's stealthy and as silent as rust.
It attacks nose and throat
You don't bleed or bloat,
So total prevention techniques are a must.

There is no magic bullet to fix this pandemic. There is no vaccine. There may never be one. We have to follow the best medical advice and adhere to the social and hygienic practises that minimise the spread of infection.

89. Hygiene

People are the problem spreading the germ,
To suppress its large spread we must be firm.
Wash your hands down
Complete without a frown
And we'll minimise this virus long term.

Chapter 21

FATIGUE

I can sense that the pressure that I am putting on myself is changing. I'm starting to question both my physical and mental wellbeing during this time of semi isolation. Is passing fellow shoppers in the supermarket without consequence? There are not many gloved and masked people there-including me. Is my plastic wrapped delivered newspaper "safe"? Gardening, painting and waving to people from afar is all very innocent and mildly humorous but there's the gnawing thoughts about all the things you want to do and the places you want to visit. But can't!

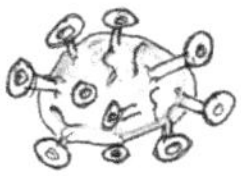

90. Limerick Fatigue

I'm sick of all the limerick "thinks",
Writing them has driven me to drinks.
Clink clickity clink
One more I do sink,
Oh! how my poor virus brain now shrinks.

Lockdown has its ups and downs. There was a time I had my share of downs. Very dark times. I'm sure everybody will go through a range of emotions at this time.

91. Counselling Required

The limerick lifeform is near at an end,
Finding word rhymes has my brain on a bend.
Virus topics are morose
Don't need another dose
And this may be the last verse I send.

It's so sad that I may be slipping into limerick depression. The worlds numbers of infections are just going up and up. Heavy.

92. Limerick Depression

I'm tired of the limerick game,
The rhyme's got to be all the same.
Brain's running low
Must let it go
Taking up knitting 'cos this lark is so lame.

This the middle of dark verse, but, it's getting lighter. I'm in the tunnel looking for the light that I know is there. This maybe our lot for a long time. Collectively and individually we have to take charge of our destiny and do what's required to reduce the viral threat.

93. Dark Verse

At home in lockdown is a curse,
Much better if you had your own nurse.
Tuck you in at night
Pleasant dreams without fright
I'll be free soon and won't need a hearse.

I feel that the cloud has lifted. I have found the tunnel and the light. A coffee and cake and a warm sunny day and feel I'm ready to capture the words that I need chasing my Covid-19 story. I think it was Irish coffee that did the trick.

94. Risen

Great joy the Limerick Phoenix has risen,
At three sheets set the sail on the mizzen.
The words are in flow
Composed from go to whoa
And I thought my verse sense was all wizen.

It's going to take more effort to fully return. "Keep Calm and Carry On" was the catch cry and its applicable in so many situations today. You need an attitude and a set of behaviours appropriate for this new set of social norms. We need to help each other.

95. Relapse

A young man tried to write a good limerick,
The words came out funny and didn't stick.
He said with a frown
This can't go down
I'll have to sharpen my pencil that's the trick.

Getting back takes effort. Anything worthwhile takes effort. I like the Nike expression – "Just Do It". How about "Carry On and Just Do It"

96. Hallelujah

Hallelujah I've seen the light
And not seeming to be too trite,
The rhymes are back
Jumped over the crack
Checked in for the long limerick fight.

I've had no helpers to get it together again. All is well and I'm feeling positive about the situation.

97. Helper

I've put pen to paper and I'm back.
No beer, wine or a whisky mac.
There's a rhyme shine,
The words are all fine
And not even with a whiskey they call Jack.

I felt like I was kidnapped. The superheroes of tiredness, depression, loneliness and alcohol all played a part with my mind set for a while. I liken it to being captured by a huge cloud of influence. When you are within the cloud it's hard to see through it. My cloud was only thin, misty and small but I needed to have it blown away.

98. Ransom

Don't pay the ransom I've escaped,
They made me say "I'm finished" those caped.
It wasn't me
I had to flee,
Now the limericks are true and not aped.

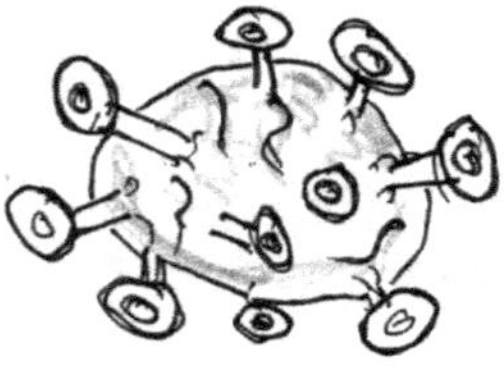

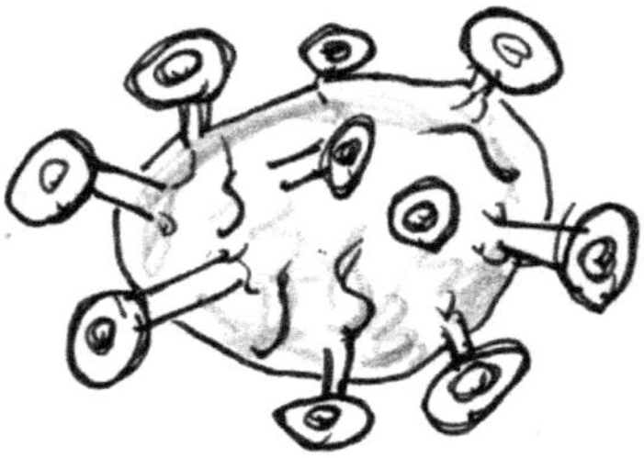

Chapter 22

RECOVERY

We now understand the fight we have with Covid-19. We need a calm and quiet set of actions. Stay at home – particularly if you're in the older age group. Send kids to school because they seem to be largely unaffected by the virus.

We must find out how many people are infected who and where they are. They can be put in isolation and treated. The statistics gathered gives an overall measure of the population progress. Are we winning which is shown by the graph of the infected flattening. Believe in the maths.

If you have cough like symptoms of sneezing, a temperature and a runny nose, get yourself tested and if you prove to be positive for the virus, stay isolated for fourteen days.

99. Take a Test

Take a test and maybe you're alright,
If not isolate for a fortnight.
Don't be a fuss,
Do it for us
And we'll give Covid-19 a fright.

Understanding the numbers is the key to our knowledge of success.

100. Understanding

We now understand the fight,
The virus now is not such a fright.
We keep it at bay
Each and every day
As our sensible actions knock it out of sight.

You can stay in lockdown or exercise a degree of safe separation and journey to a close sunny place even though the safe place is only in your mind.

101. Sunshine

It's great to be out in the sun.
Easing lockdown from uncertainty has begun.
Feeling very light,
The sunshine is bright
And it's a credit to all we have done.

The leaders in some parts of the world are fairly average in their leadership to control Covid-19. Some, on occasions have endorsed actions that have been absolutely downright dangerous. I believe some are responsible for making the situation worse by allowing practices that increased the number of infected people.

102. Politicians Won

Our pollies have been setting the pace,
Brilliant decisions and directions are ace.
Called the right shots
Connected all the dots
To knock the invasive virus off base.

All the petty bickering and slanging matches have halted. Most politicians who are at last behaving well, for now, deserve the "Honourable" tag in front of their names.

103. Politicians Two

Most politicians are at last worth their salt,
Making great decisions without any fault.
We owe a great debt
For the results they get
'Cos they're causing the virus to halt.

Our health, safety and wellbeing is heavily reliant on groups I will call health workers. Included in the group are Nurses and Doctors as well as cleaners and aged care workers. These are people who work diligently at their jobs, generally without public acknowledgement and usually without great monetary reward.

104. Health Workers

Health workers are nothing but gold,
Selfless actions saving young and old.
They step up every day
Without executive pay
They're our treasures formed from a unique mould.

We are now emerging from the cloud that is Covid-19. The cloud surrounded us all. We all operated within the ground level cloud. The cloud lifted and shifted. It became an umbrella. There were still restraints on our activities but there was a degree of freedom to behave safely under the ever-present cover.

105. The Cloud

It's great to emerge from out of the cloud,
No longer housebound, distressed and cowed.
Virus counts are slain
Medicos advised well again.
Of the health workers make we all feel so proud.

Staying positive – acting positive – doing positive things. Until there is a vaccine the virus will be with us. Think safe – be safe – do safe.

106. All Positive

Life ahead is a positive view,
Taking direction from a medicos' cue.
The sun's warm and bright
Pushing away the night
Forging right ahead without even a blue.

Visits are now on again. Small groups and some degree of social distancing is required. Some people play fast and loose with the requirements, but most follow the spirit of the game.

107. Together Again

Making contacts with the grandkids again,
No longer apart with separation pain.
The visits are on
Restrictions are gone
Happiness all round again will now reign.

Pubs are open. First was service only at widey separated tables. Now you can have a drink standing at the bar.

108. Beers

Having a beer with your mates is now on,
A lot of the restrictions are now gone.
Future's great but limited
Efforts from all are spirited.
Are we now facing a new confident dawn?

With great leadership we have great followship. As stated, we are controlling our own fate. Follow and believe in the science.

109. Home

At home the virus recovery is great,
Control was won by leaders of this state.
Living with the virus
Is successful by us,
We are now controlling our own fate.

Chapter 23

SUCCESS

Small practises will ensure successful living with the virus. Testing in great numbers is invaluable in detecting the level of infection in community. Continuous testing in large numbers gives us knowledge. Some world leaders suggest the opposite!

110. Success

We must live with the virus and control it.
Smart practises will prevent the virus hit.
Lives will be smart,
Lived with strong heart
Because the community we all live in is close knit.

Understand the virus. Understand how to measure it in a community. Ensure safe practises by all. This is the minimum because lives matter.

111. Lives Matter

The Corona Virus takes a back seat
When overwhelmed by the king of the tweet.
All lives matter
Whoever the batter
"Cos balancing it all is a great feat.

We may be living with Covid-19 for some time. I believe it will take a vaccine to control it much the same way we control Polio, Measles, Mumps, Rubella and so on. Even if we develop a vaccine there will people who, for various reasons, will flat out refuse to take it. I believe in vaccination but it's your choice and our consequence.

112. The Future

Life now is different and yet the same,
We've changed forever since the virus came.
We now show respect
Society is not wrecked
Do we really have to find blame?

And finally. Words fail me.

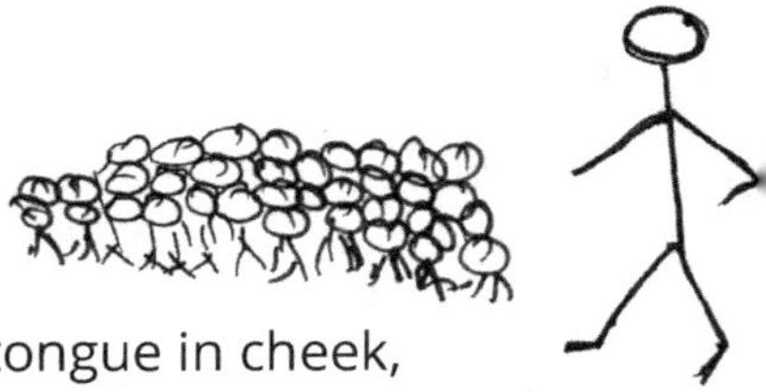

113. Sarcastic

He can be sarcastic with tongue in cheek,
The true virus numbers he doesn't want to seek.
Stop all the tests
Our numbers will be best
And we'll show all the deaths are of the weak.

How I tried to do it.

114. Limericks For All

A limerick is a complete package of words,
Short and entertaining even for nerds.
The rhythms are tight,
The images bright
With rhyming in doubles and thirds.

Or $\frac{2}{5}$ & $\frac{3}{5}$ or 40% & 60% or $\int_1^5 \mathit{limerick.BS}$

The words I tried to use.

115 Limerick Form

Limericks can be quaint, Irish or rude,
But not when handled by this dude.
They're punchy and strong
Just ripping along
With interesting yarns that are not crude.

I hope you enjoyed my journey through Covid-19. I do live in the most isolated Capital City in the most isolated island country in the world – Perth, Western Australia. All our "infections" were from returning travellers or visiting ships. Our journey is sincere as is our empathy for the plight of the world.

And as a final word to the nay sayers and general non believers.....

116. It's Real

People who appear loud, confident and thick,
They steer the truth away real quick.
The virus is real,
Re-direct your zeal
And help us give Covid-19 the flick.

P.S.

There has to be a P.S.

117. P.S. No B.S.
I'll finish the tome with a P.S.,
No big words, no images, no BS.
The writing's all done,
I'll now impress no one
'Cos I've drained my poor brain to X.S.

And finally, finally – I couldn't resist. For the politicians of the world who don't accept the pandemic is real and that it is responsible for great numbers suffering from the disease and the many thousands who have lost their lives. Good people will see us through this Covid-19 Pandemic. Apologies to Percy Bysshe Shelley's Ozimandias.

118. Polimandias Tweet

Polimandias put out the first tweet,
Chiselled on a pedestal under his feet.
"All should give praise
For the virus I raze
It's Covid-19 and I have it all beat."

ADDENDUM

Covid-19 is here. It's with all of us worldwide. To some it's a nuisance, to some it's a distraction, to some it's debilitating and to some it's a death sentence. To all of us it's a great concern and cooperation between governments, health advisors and every person on the planet is required.

We know what to do. Personal hygiene and social practises have been outlined for many months. Governments should know how to orchestrate rules and behaviour guidelines for their constituents. Some are better at this than others.

We need a world united.

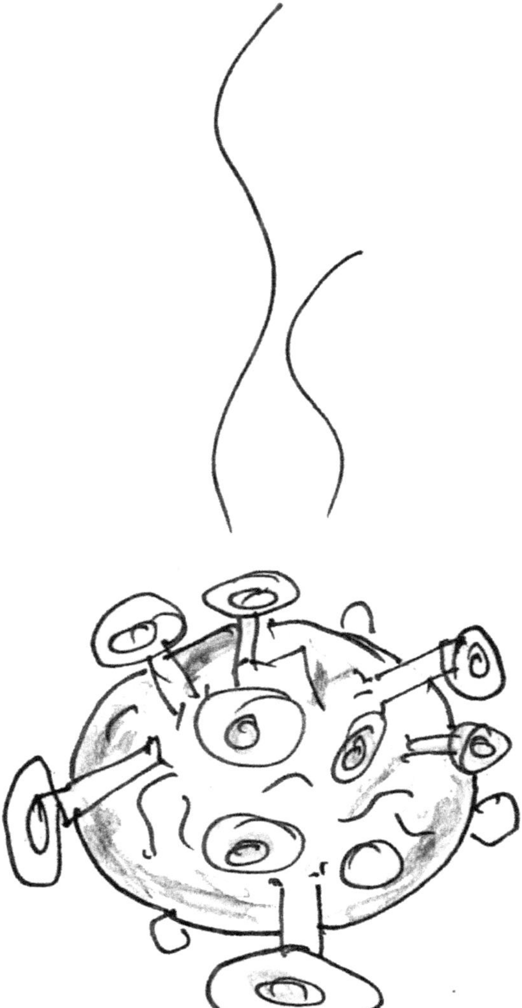

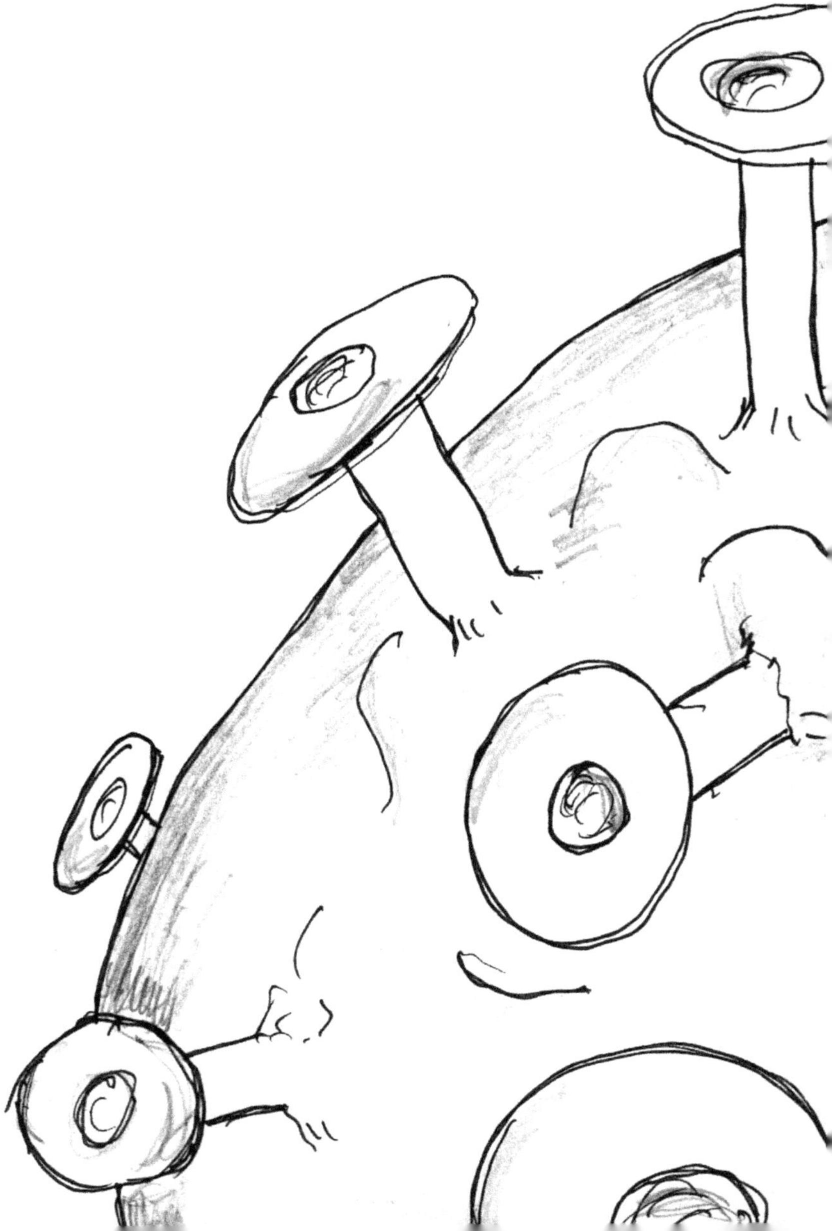

www.ingramcontent.com/pod-product-compliance
Lightning Source LLC
Chambersburg PA
CBHW071409290426
44108CB00014B/1747
9780645089202